Roadrunners AND Sandwich Terns

EXPLORING BIRDS WITH CHILDREN

by

SUZANNE SAMSON

illustrated by

PRESTON NEEL

Roberts Rinehart Publishers
Boulder, Colorado

SUZANNE SAMSON
To the looney members of my family.
And to my girls,
Winter and Summer

PRESTON NEEL
For Magnolia Shand Neel

Text Copyright © 1997 Suzanne Samson

Illustrations copyright © 1997 Preston Neel

International Standard Book Number 1-57098-129-9

Library of Congress Catalog Card Number 97-65652

Published by Roberts Rinehart Publishers

5455 Spine Road, Boulder, Colorado 80301

Published in the U.K. and Ireland by

Roberts Rinehart Publishers

Trinity House, Charleston Road

Dublin 6, Ireland

Distributed to the trade by Publishers Group West.

Printed in Hong Kong

Grab your binoculars and let's go bird watching!

Discover birds soaring and gliding with ease,

Hovering near flowers and nesting in trees,

Or find them in water wading up to their knees.

Now adjust the focus and
you might notice...

Sandpipers playing a jig,

A Loon dancing with a pig,

A Cowbird flying over the moon,

A Redhead in the Longbranch Saloon,

Gray Catbirds perched in
a tree,

Surfbirds riding waves in the sea,

Yellowlegs wearing
panty hose,

A Red Footed Booby
polishing toes,

Sandwich Terns
discussing a sub,

Laughing Gulls at a comedy club,

A soaring Kite
snagged by a twig,

A Bald Eagle in
need of a wig,

Snowy Owls
riding a sleigh,

A Cardinal tagging
out a Jay,

A Tattler beginning to cry,

Nutcrackers shelling
nuts for a pie,

Sapsuckers slurping a treat,

Roadrunners racing down the street,

Trumpeter Swans blasting through air, or

Stilts overlooking the fair.

Now change the focus and be objective.
Look at the world from a bird's perspective!

Least Sandpiper

Calidris minutilla

Size: about 6 inches

Habitat: beaches, marshes, mudflats, bays and estuaries

This bird is commonly found in wet habitats. Its call is a piercing *creet* or *creep* sound.

Red-throated Loon

Gavia stellata

Size: about 24–26 inches

Habitat: coastal waters, inshore waters

The Red-throated Loon is the smallest loon and is the only one that can fly directly from water. Other loons need a running start. Males and females are similar in appearance.

Bronzed Cowbird

Molothrus aeneus

Size: about 8 inches

Habitat: open areas with brush, residential locations

The Bronzed Cowbird, previously known as the Red-eyed Cowbird, can be found foraging in large flocks. Its call is a low, husky *chuk* sound.

Gray Catbird

Dumetella carolinensis

Size: about 8½ inches

Habitat: brushy areas, residential areas, along meadows and streams

The Gray Catbird is often difficult to see because it hides in dense thickets. Its song is a combination of melodious, squeaky and harsh notes. Some mimic the songs of other birds. Its call is a *mew* sound.

Redhead

Aythya americana

Size: about 19 inches

Habitat: marshes and inshore waters

This diving duck usually eats at night, feeding on aquatic plant life. The male has a catlike call.

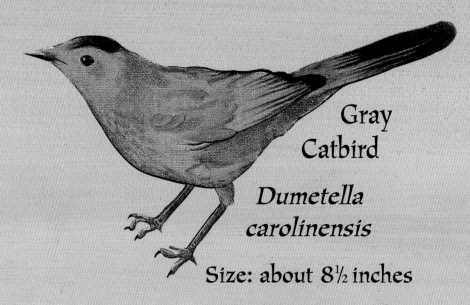

Surfbird

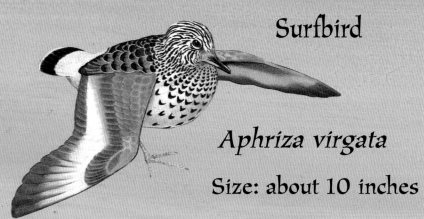

Aphriza virgata

Size: about 10 inches

Habitat: rocky seashores

The Surfbird, a quiet bird, can be found in flocks of up to three dozen. While flying, it sometimes has a *kee-weak* call.

Greater Yellowlegs

Tringa melanoleuca

Size: about 14 inches

Habitat: mudflats, shores, salt marshes, freshwater areas

This large sandpiper is a tall, wading shorebird that often bobs its head. Its call is a shrill *tyew-tyew-tyew* sound.

Red Footed Booby

Sula sula

Size: about 28 inches

Habitat: islands, tropical oceans

The smallest of the boobies, the Red Footed Booby is quick and graceful. It can be found pursuing flying fish and seizing them in the air. This tropical bird often follows fishing boats or ships for several days.

Sandwich Tern

Sterna sandvicensis

Size: about 15 inches

Habitat: beaches, coastal inshore waters

Sandwich Terns are the only terns whose black beaks have yellow tips. They can be found nesting in colonies on sandy beaches or diving for fish.

Laughing Gull

Larus atricilla

Size: about 16½ inches

Habitat: beaches, coastal marshes, mudflats

The Laughing Gull feeds on flying insects and nests in colonies. It is common along the eastern coast. Its call is a high pitched laugh: *ha-ha-ha-ha-haaaa.*

Mississippi
Kite

*Ictinia
mississippiensis*

Size: about 14½ inches

Habitat: grasslands, open woods

This graceful hawk usually feeds on flying insects, but it also captures lizards, frogs and mice.

Bald Eagle

Haliaeetus leucocephalus

Size: from 30 to 42 inches

Habitat: bays and estuaries, reservoirs, rivers and lakes

Bald Eagles build large nests out of sticks in tall trees. They use their nests for several years. The Bald Eagle feeds primarily on fish, but also eats carrion, small mammals and injured waterfowl. Its call is a squeaky chatter.

Snowy Owl

Nyctea scandiaca

Size: about 23 inches

Habitat: grasslands and open areas, shores, marshes

The Snowy Owl nests on the ground and primarily feeds on lemmings, but it also consumes small rodents.

Wandering Tattler

Heteroscelus incanus

Size: about 11 inches

Habitat: rocky coasts, beaches

The Wandering Tattler's call is several short, rapid whistles. It usually makes its call right before it begins to fly.

Northern Cardinal

Cardinalis cardinalis

Size: about 9 inches

Habitat: woodlands, thickets, residential locations

The Northern Cardinal feeds on insects, grain, seeds and fruit. It does not migrate and its song, a clear whistle with many variations, can be heard almost year-round.

Clark's Nutcracker

Nucifraga columbiana

Size: about 12 inches

Habitat: western mountain regions, coniferous forests

The Clark's Nutcracker feeds on insects and pine seeds. Its call is a nasal *craaa*. This bird can store several nuts in a cheek pouch under its tongue in addition to the nuts it holds in its beak.

Greater Roadrunner

Geococcyx californianus

Size: about 23 inches

Habitat: grasslands, deserts, arid woodlands

The Greater Roadrunner is a big, ground-dwelling cuckoo that is often seen running swiftly with its neck outstretched. This shy bird seldom flies. It eats insects, snakes, lizards, small birds and rodents. The Roadrunner's song consists of many *coos*.

Red-naped Sapsucker

Sphyrapicus nuchalis

Size: about 8½ inches

Habitat: western mountain coniferous forests, aspen groves

This medium-sized woodpecker feeds on sap that comes from small holes the bird drills in bark. It also eats the insects that are attracted to the sap.

Black-necked Stilt

Himantopus mexicanus

Size: about 14 inches

Habitat: marshes, lakes, mudflats, and along tidal shores

The Black-necked Stilt wades deeper than most shorebirds because of its long legs.

Trumpeter Swan

Cygnus buccinator

Size: about 60 inches

Habitat: lakes and rivers, tundra marshes, bays

Flocks of migrating Trumpeter Swans usually travel in formation. Their call is a series of low pitched *honks*.

REFERENCES

Stephen Whitney. *The Audubon Society Nature Guides, Western Forests.* New York: Alfred A. Knopf, Inc., 1985.

Bayard H. McConnaughey and Evelyn McConnaughey. *National Audubon Society Nature Guides, Pacific Ocean.* New York: Alfred A. Knopf, Inc., 1985.

John Farrand, Jr. *An Audubon Handbook, Eastern Birds.* New York: McGraw-Hill Book Company, 1988.

John Farrand, Jr. *An Audubon Handbook, Western Birds.* New York: McGraw-Hill Book Company, 1988.

Roger Tory Peterson. *The Peterson Field Guide Series, A Field Guide to the Birds East of the Rockies.* Maps by Virginia Marie Peterson. Boston: Houghton Mifflin Company, 1980.

Miklos D.F. Udvardy. *The Audubon Society Field Guide to North American Birds, Western Region.* Visual Key by Susan Rayfield. New York: Alfred A. Knopf, Inc., 1977.

National Geographic Society Field Guide to the Birds of North America. Washington: National Geographic Society, 1983.

Richard J. Chandler. *The Facts On File Field Guide to North Atlantic Shorebirds.* New York, Oxford: Facts On File, 1989.